VITAL PURSUITS

VITAL PURSUITS

Evan Glasson

H_NGM_N BKS
www.h-ngm-nbks.com

FIRST H_NGM_N EDITION, November 2011

ISBN 978-0-9832215-4-8

Book and cover design by Nate Pritts and Scott O'Connor
Cover photo © pavelsvoboda

CONTENTS

FOR MY FAMILY

VITAL PURSUITS

Edwin Budding invented the lawnmower.

Read all 44 Sonnets from the Portuguese

aloud to self, was jealous of Mrs. Browning.

Somewhere beneath the wilting

or flowering, the grass is green.

I want to be being in action. Tree limbs

grow through a chain linked

fence. Drawing a sword,

I could never quite capture the glint.

On a road in Chile, we

dropped our bags, sprinted

toward an active volcano. Would have cost

too much to climb. The dog digs

and digs. There's nothing there. The dog digs.

As the road gets longer it appears

to narrow. Too narrow. Two narrow

boats on a river in Providence.

The bridge I have never seen

down is not down. Bet it's been down.

In one of the intervals I was away,

I was a way to be believable

as the conception of myself I imagined would have

imagined. The best Chagall paintings mend

floating people to happy corners out of the blue

background. These images mark the months

of mother's year. My mother Mary.

My mother who loves Jesus and is sad

when her children are home and she is going alone

to Mass. Molecule is Latin

for little mass. I count my blessings

in blades of uncut grass, sing

praises. Glass in the name

of the father. The wave's

strength is measured by its breaking.

Mother's mother died in a car crash.

The round specks of wind-

shield, the road, the glisten. Listen,

I understood everything she said

except her insistence I did not understand,

which was everything.

•   •   •

Needles pushed into a pillow
shaped like the planet.
All eyes look out.
I am the camel
trying to take Jesus up
on his offer. Through
and through, it's been
rough. Down boy,
down. Stay. The dog listens
only to the woman
who is the hand legs lips brain bliss
that feeds him. Friends
don't understand how I eat
so much. What can I say—
I am *always* hungry. Knead less
and the bread will be lighter,
the recipe advises. Head full
of compatriot sway,

the drunk at the all-night diner
tries to pick a fight with me.
The waitress delivers his
Belgian waffle with strawberries,
bananas, and whipped cream.
A bit of cruelty's a necessity.
If I didn't shorten the leash,
he would waste the whole day
looking for the best place to go.

.　　.　　.

Posing a higher risk
of death than sky
diving or motorcycling: rock
climbing. Ever an optimist,
the scientist thought he could
mold urine into gold.
Up or down, not between.

It was phosphorous

they had in common.

From the Greek, meaning light.

So highly reactive,

it's never a free element

in nature. High speeds

into the wind trumps

grabbing onto sediment not

there. Sentiment: I am

suited for a queen.

At the turn I hold.

I hold at the river.

Christin, I want to hold

my hand in my hand

(unconscious of either)

over the button of your pants

as we look out

on the Great Salt River.

Ether: an inaccurate explanation

for how light moves across

the emptiness of space.

Shed skin and it's lost.

Shed light and it's gained.
Shed scales for scales
bright black.
Father had an old shed
filled with tools
I was not
taught how to operate.

• • •

Galileo measured moon mountains
by measuring the shadows
they cast. Before going out to sea,
the old man says: It is better
to be lucky. But
I would rather be exact. Then
when luck comes you are ready.
The point of view
is what gets me. Surrounded

by salt water and super thirsty.

If I don't play in at least one

NBA game in the next two years,

as per the contract signed in 1991

and since tucked in mother's desk,

I will owe my brother one hundred dollars.

Quit so close, as Jennifer says,

to quiet. Galileo went blind in 1637.

The year seems random

but one plus six is seven—

three numbers. The point of distance

is the stance it requires and creates.

It's always bugged me how

when there's an even number of objects,

no one can be at the center.

.   .   .

We begin by claiming a color.

I call blue. She says I cannot

be blue, she is already blue.

Left my lamp beside the golden door,

visited a town in Haiti

I can only mispronounce:

Grow, mourn. I can only miss,

pronounce: the more grown, the less

left. Groan. In a new place, the dog

sniffs everything he can get his nose on.

Ezra said less is more.

Walt said more or less.

Evan said no then no, yes, yes.

How can I explain being defined

by indecision, I thought.

Then seconds guessed myself.

Gilt: thin layer of gold on the surface.

Guilt: that muck beneath the surface.

The tasted fruit does not keep long.

The parking meters hiss:

for every moment you stay,

you must pay, you must pay.

Bigger the space, bigger the heating bill.

Peddling in others' affairs,

my legs tired. I spoke

of the frame and the tread.

Takes forever to balance

when constantly fearful of falling.

Bad paint job in this apartment:

patience, patience.

•   •   •

New York: the greatest everything

bagel with cream cheese

I have ever tasted. Her being

in Boston: the whole at its center.

Holey, holy, wholly Lord,

nod of maybe or might.

The night my friends and I

drank and sang Sinatra and loved

poetry but forgot how

hurt we had to have been

to love it. Cummings says feeling is first

then thought creeps in at the close.

Then thought creeps in at the close.

Cheap mattress an incline

down which I cannot help

but slide. Fourth grade, science teacher

said, uphill, go side to side.

Twelve years later,

Katherine asked which road

I take to get where I want to go.

The short. You fall

in love quickly, she said.

What about going home?

Going home? I most likely

probably end up taking the longer road, I said.

You fall out of love slowly, she said,

keeps saying. Top two

international destinations for U.S. travelers?

Mexico and Canada. We are travelers.

If I am anything I am

an apple eager to fall

father from the tree. I speak of building

because it is both motion and stasis.

I speak of level because it is

a destroying balancing endlessly

balancing destroying.

When I was a boy, I hated onions.

They were all I could taste.

Walking on Hope Street, Christin

tightens her grip on my fingers,

says she is sorry.

• • •

All I had to do was keep turning
left, said the winner
of the racecar race.
Modesty is admirable until it turns
into gross inaccuracy. By gross I mean
the bulk of it. The disgusting.
The whole before any gets taken
away. Who are we to turn our heads
so quickly? The sound trailing the sight.
Palindromes make me think
some things really are the same
no matter how you look at them
most things change.
Life, friends, is the pits.
Our wheels pop off.
We are put back together
and on our way again.
I want to champion so many things:

The consideration of others
on the road that is not a road
and their compliant consideration
of us. The overt sponsorship.
The merging and the weaving.
The mother on the blue-gray carpet,
daughter between her knees.
The braiding of hair.
The mesh cap of the father,
the round belly balancing the flat beer.

  •   •   •

A telephone pole covered
with stapled down flyers.
So much to do,
little that interests me.
It is necessary to have such markers,
grounders of all this energy.

If you want to talk

we can talk. Researchers have found

a strong link between practitioner

empathy and the duration

of the common cold. We know trauma

victims' length and intensity of suffering

is contingent upon the reaction

of the first person they share

that suffering with. We try

to forget, remember, endure

each year upon the ever

increasing complication

of birthday candles. I wish I'd need not

keep secret my secret (Of, of, of…).

I want breathing room and you

closer than physically possible.

Dryer sheet meets pant

leg in the tumbling ever

after. Here is the scary thing:

static goes the electricity.

From together to peeling

apart. Here is the scary thing:

In the 1930s, gangsters called

the machine gun a Chicago piano.

One person's idea

of music can be the instrument

in the other's murdering.

Bespeaking the trench in our coats:

Callousness may be fashionable

enough for future generations

to emulate, but if you aren't feeling well

today I'm sorry. I am so, so sorry.

•   •   •

The point of the parade

is the cymbals,

shining in their crashing.

Given this coming and going—

fathers, shuttles, lovers—

steady alteration, of course,

is all we can count on.

Altar: sacramental space.

Into the suggestion box,

I dropped everything

I've ever been,

hoping to be chosen, held, read

aloud by someone else

in such an order as to

formulate a more accurate

current self. Skyscrapers were

made viable

with the invention of the elevator.

With the ups and downs,

should there be great heights,

we must be able to reach them.

If I am an instrument,

I am the tuba.

Awkward heft. The highest notes

know depth. Never go alone.

This is rule number one

of scuba. There is also the pressure,

the awareness of how distance between

base and brim correlates

to the rate at which we move

within. We have so much

to learn of brittle stars.

During the dive,

we should adjust our buoyancy,

move with currents where possible.

We must remember to stay close

to our companions.

   •   •   •

Two towns in Arkansas

share the name Evening Shade.

Here, take it.

I do not understand. Leaving

the luminescent dark,

we arrive at the luminescent

dark. Grandfather died.

Rector told me

church and school

were built in the early twenties.

An undecided

major swaying

half drunk from bash

to bash, all lit up

by black light. I am drawn

to the crooked of her teeth.

For accuracy's sake: the light

appears purple. Many colors

constitute a black eye.

The guy who didn't get punched

calls it a shiner.

The Problem of Pain

quiet on mother's shelf.

I take it down.

I open it. The Problem of Pain

is we feel it,

know others feel it worse,

and this brings us comfort.

Lying together on the couch,

Christin says she is uncomfortable.

I fear she means it

so many ways. The dog frets.

The dog cries. He wants

to bury the bone,

can't get outside himself.

• • •

Dandelion origins: tooth of lion.

Queen of my jumbled jungle,

gouge me of sloth tendency,

gorge me with cat certainty.

The mathematician said rise

over run. I thought of codependency,

of ways to take off.

The winning thoroughbred, Cigar,

was named after an aviation checkpoint

not a tobacco product.

Given the choice of flying

or burning, even terrified-

of-heights-I choose flying.

Ready for takeoff, all systems go.

In Spanish, the word for pigeon

and dove is the same.

Beautiful-ugly-pesky-lovely—

all this being up in the air.

The old man came in from the cold.

I am looking for something

to feed my wife, he said. When he left

I nearly wept for proximity,

for spoon on ceramic, for half-parted

lips exhaling, for bread

hardened but unbroken. I nearly wept

for you, future Christin, old and sick,

but mostly for me—always mostly

for me—not driving around Providence

on a cold night to find you

whatever it is you might not want.

The Japanese word for death

is pronounced like the English word she.

This is also how to say poem.

•   •   •

Scientists have discovered

blue makes us

more creative; red, more cautious.

Timid stepping onto the tightrope

toward companionship, he juggled

telephone, ocean, papaya

as he walked.

In other languages, animals

make other sounds. Regardless,

the red calls out

to the curious blue

morning—We rise. Monochromatic

attire an attempt to curb the clashing.

For years I thought *curb* was *curve.*

To perform feats

never before or henceforth performed,
I turn, walk, turn.
Wore all brown yesterday, felt like shit.
Felt like dirt. Felt like a perennial
of the brightest blue blooming.
Alexander Graham Bell muffled
his finest invention
to work without interruption. Blue
stifling blue.

     •   •   •

Sorry is a board game
we play with her daughter.
Headstones are given
to veterans for free.
I'm blue, they say in unison.
Bored isn't the same
as tired. To be tired

is to lack motivation.

The tire spins, spins, and spins.

We draw cards.

Sometimes when brother plays

music, I think I should be

playing music. We make moves.

Christin in high boots and a dress,

the sunlight through the fabric,

her body's silhouette.

Sometimes I want to hold

you like a grown man

on the breast of the woman

so unsure if she loves him

that she weeps at his fragility.

Pulling into the gas station,

we ran out of gas. Whose responsibility?

Grandfather, a submarine operator

during the war

with a fondness for marigolds—

the man not the war—smeared peach

bonbons on

my shut lips that day in the cabin.

Annulment: it never happened.

A null meant: Christin,

awful as the awful has been,

do you know what it is

to never have happened? What to love

about sunken ships:

the massive floating required prior.

Sometimes everything

seems an airy appendage. The martyr says

give me the guillotine

if it means motion at the severance.

•   •   •

Middle school,

the assignment was to make

a shoebox imaginary.

Behind the immensity

of Styrofoam stone, Sisyphus was

a paper doll held together by a toothpick.

The gods were nowhere.

Nothing was to scale.

Even the original is a replication.

When the child comes home

charged with the task of depicting

Eskimo life, she is wise enough

to make appear immersed

the whale's tale. Buried

beast, boat, spears, people bundled up,

cellophane water blue as it is clear.

A friend listens to sad music

because she is sad. A house of ice

to stay warm in.

The child wants no help.

Painstaking, such work is.

One by one, she builds

an igloo out of Domino sugar cubes.

·   ·   ·

The actors wore yak hair costumes

for their roles in Cats.

He once wanted so badly to be

what she wanted

he ended up being

neither himself nor the thing

he thought she wanted.

In the coat of a lesser known being,

refusing domesticity,

he came to know his grief

internationally. I dream

Christin has an emotional affair

with William Carlos Williams.

I dream I have

to park a school bus

in a space that won't fit

a Prism. I dream awake

I am light—infinite

color, clean lines, perfect

shape. We bought the cheapest

pottery set. Wobbly spin. I am

interested in anything

that doesn't end where it begins.

Took until now to realize:

Self, be always becoming.

This is never unbecoming.

My friend, the foreigner,

wrote of her waste but meant waist.

Curve of presence, heap of absence,

that steel and wood

that would steal the track

from under us. After grandfather died—

no lie—I became unable

to love. Regardless or because

of this desire to stay here,

I find myself forever tethered

to words like evanescence

which whisper: go on, disappear.

·　　·　　·

The cruise ship crew

tries to corral for karaoke.

A little older now,

a little more self-conscious,

we resist these commands

to sing the song of another,

relish resemblance.

Just because I told her hold my hand

she would not hold my hand.

Days later, she says maybe

she'd be better with a masculine

incapable of poem writing.

I have never been aboard a Carnival

Cruise—thank God, Jah, Allah, science,

some higher being, all this energy, nothing.

I hear the filth

is overwhelming. So many fingers

in the same salad bar.

The can becomes empty

then connected to another can

by twice knotted string. The preserves

get better and better

until they go bad. I want

to tell you so many things.

I think I can I think I can. Childishly,

the modes of going away keep coming

back. Blue man drank silver nitrate

to dye his skin. A bright spot

on the bored walk:

attention granted when sought.

Don't worry. I won't go that far.

One color spins into another.

Our love, too, like a Ferris wheel.

Up and down going round.

Scarier though—the time we were at the top

and the ride suddenly stopped.

The whole park was visible

from where we sat,

you gripping my wrist,

I hate the feeling of being trapped.

In the middle of the carnival

is a game called Shoot the Idiot.

A man runs around

a fenced-in field.

Beebe guns that look like real guns

point at him. Each pellet—

hit or miss—is a well-rounded opportunity

to be one thing or another.

I feel nauseous and entertained.

   •   •   •

In the first season's theme song,

the Professor and Mary Anne

were mentioned as *all the rest*

on Gilligan's Island.

She came to be the beauty

dressed in the everyday;

he, the brains that couldn't figure

out how to be saved. The fool's namesake

is an archipelago. Every land

is an island—

some are moved to become one

with others. Ardor refuses order.

When my mind-bus

stops on the avenue of experience,

let the doors open

to the first warm day of April

and young, thin women

without sleeves. Let all

fares be free. Let me

walk toward you as you

walk toward me. You are the quietest

step of the lioness. Heard,

the gazelles scatter. Innate

or learned, pause yields claws.

I am coming to meet you,

darling. In the close-up

from the director's cut,

a golden expanse narrows

into the graceful collapse

to the beast on my back.

I twitch and shake.

I twitch and shake

and tilt my saved face.

Filling your flesh with my flesh,

your hunger with my heart,

I succumb to becoming

brains and bones. I pray:

May the hyenas, vultures,

and all the rest come soon.

•   •   •

You could give me the seeds

of a thousand vegetables, a lot of land,

the sun and rain, and still

I might starve to death.

This is what it means

to have been raised

in the suburbs then chosen

the cities. When Sitting Bull

was murdered, his people went

to Wounded Knee.

Of course I have no right.

Yet I witnessed

Christin yesterday brought to the floor

as if praying for a root canal.

The origin is in the water,

in mothers working many jobs

and sons complaining

about burnt grilled cheese.

The child I live with wants Wonder

Bread, but I buy the whole grain.

Someday she will understand

why we ought to opt

for such variance in color and texture.

Do not forgive me, mother, for I have lived.

It has been ten years since my last Confession.

Second grade, Sister required

we think about every word

when reciting the rosary. I got stuck

on *In the name* for what seemed

like forever. The bare bulb,

the puddle in the basement,

me, seven years old

in the middle

of it, barefoot and weeping.

Who am I to thank

for being here? The fact of the matter

is, is a few years later

I wrote a girl wearing a wind

breaker, I like you on a rubber band

and the tiny script became legible

in that opening of saintly hands.

In Spanish, *adiós* means *goodbye*

and *a Dios* means *to God*.

In A Clean, Well-lighted Place,

father and other words are replaced

with *nada*, which means *nothing*

and thereby, something.

My version would exchange

the empty for everything.

Todo: to do, and do, and do and do,

mindful of my gratitude.
Sister, we must not let
our habits hide so much.
I took Innocent as my Confirmation
name. I keep it and give it back.
Oh, to be both there and by
at the same time. Of Mice and Men
is the title of a book I read then
but what I remember
most is the potential for rabbits.
Litter: one man's garbage is another's
abundance of unbearably adorable.

•   •   •

They were perfectly fine
windows aside from the fact
that they had no walls
to hold them. When Buzz ended—

Forget them. To hold you, Christin.—

When Buzz ended

up on the moon, he played

Sinatra's Fly Me to the Moon.

I cut out last year's lovers

from the Chagall calendar

belonging to mother,

rubber-cemented them to the panes.

Correction: they needed

a framed absence.

I am six years old.

Reminded: Don't go

so far you forget

you're already there.

Can you hear me,

father? You were already

there. The time I kissed

her kissed her kissed her,

leapt up to turn on the light.

Re-minded: There are many

moons. Heavy with want

for narrowing and opening

to meet like mouths

begun at opposite ends

of the same spaghetti.

I am six years old.

Every story worth hearing

is a variation of

Lady and the Tramp. Love,

love is confetti: fun bursts

into a clean up

that's hardly ever done.

Father, today is my birthday.

I am twenty-nine years old.

Father, this is the day I was born.

•   •   •

In the caves of Slovenia

lives a creature called the olm.

He retains his juvenile form

into adulthood. At the wedding, I love
how little the lovers need say.
Sometimes it's more about being there.
In cases of direct currents, we measure
electrical resistance in ohms.
There, there, says the mother
to the crier. There is a distance
implied. An instruction to leave it
where it is, to leave it alone.
Spanish has one word for faraway
there and another for not so
far *there*. Friend (may I call you
friend?), they've begun
hanging advertisements
underground in succession
so the train's movement
and our resistance to it makes
a combination of images one reel.
We are objects in motion that must stay
in motion. Crashing will remind us
less we forget. Yotam is at it again,
writing poems about a man

wandering the desert.

I say, this one is about me.

No, he says, it's about me.

The animal's most impressive

quality is its ability to adapt

to a life of total darkness,

the host declares.

But if that is all it has ever

known…Jesus too was

a desert wanderer. Bless a woman

in tights! Such clinging is divinest sense.

Yet every time a stranger

sits beside me I grovel.

I know something in me is

to blame or better

explain this desire to be one ample

roomed observer. I know lonely, curious

people routinely get lost

in mansions. I also know others

crowd into thatch roofed huts

with the ones they love,

deserving a different aspect of our sympathy.

Sometimes I think I feel

empathy for father. Both on be-

half of and toward

to ward off any dark hallway's

jingling keys. In Queensland,

Australia, tourists are advised

not to sit on the backs of

nor put their hands in

the mouths of crocodiles.

I thought they would open all

at once, I say of her mother's bouquet.

The child asks if I am good

in science. I tell her I am not

good in science. The nervous is the master

controlling and communicating

system of the body. I do not

remember the difference

between the pharynx and larynx,

like how they sound together though.

There was a time I knew,

but I don't know. About the tourists

and the crocodiles, she says

it's kind of stupid

but sometimes people forget

things that should be obvious.

Better safe than sorry, I guess, she says.

You pick flowers, so they're dying, then

they bloom. We make a list of stuff

we do not understand,

stick it on the fridge. Because

it is often harder to be jilter than jilted,

I am straggler at yet

another party. A friend asks

what I think the saddest noise

in the world. There is so much potential,

but I sound off on

the whack of a gavel. We are sentenced

to be set free. Honor is be holding

responsibility. Gravel in our shoes,

we persist like prisoners grateful

to be treading across sunlit concrete.

The agnostic is some obscure amphibian

whose land is arbitrary

certainties that separate the waters

between. Olmmmmm…

Ohmmmmm…Uhmmmmm…he meditates.

.   .   .

My stomach growls. It's like you

have another person in there,

the child says. I do not

tell her how it is harder

to breathe on the mountaintop.

How the one time I climbed

the whole way, there was a heavy

mist, gray. I envy the hummingbird,

rapid enough to appear floating,

capable of upside down

flying, peace embedded in

its name. Refrigerator chest.

The stomach makes its own noise.

I hum when I'm nervous.

The interior light stays off until
someone opens me. Someone open me.
I am trying like DeLorean doors.
So much can be explained by the simple
invention of the hinge. The fact is
Michael J. Fox is deteriorating.
He wants to be still but can't stop
shaking. I was raised on Back
to the Future (every part), on Family
Ties (beloved, knot),
on Teen Wolf (generationally
classic howl). I make the child
watch this last one with me.
It is my favorite—the story
of a boy mediocre until the inner
animal unleashes. Top dog
with pick of the litter
opts for refined inhibition
in the end. They hoist him
into the air but he demands
to be put down. The girl
there from the beginning

amidst a fickle, fickle crowd.

It is something greater than instinct

that overtakes and guides him now.

     •   •   •

The stairs make us

tired; the elevator,

claustrophobic. Inescapable,

this shortness of breath.

A long sigh of belief

in anything other than

the sighing could be

relief. The elephant, after losing

its sixth and last set

of teeth, starves to death.

I only get two chances

and am unwell

into the second. At twenty-nine

years old, the wisdom

pokes it head out

at the speaking point

then burrows into silent

flesh. The learned man recommends

extracting the crooked pearls

that will ruin the straight

row. Pull out the ors,

Yotam tells me,

and float along in the quiet

moonlight of a still pond.

Dear friend, how can I

say this? Tempests: tempests,

oceans: tempests,

oceans, dinghy. There are waves

I am unconvinced—given all

you have taught me

of science and history,

of music and people,

of places and objects unanchored—

there are waves I cannot believe

will wash upon the shore.

Will, wash upon me sure.
Desperately as they want
discovered, held, understood, felt,
there are messages
bottled up, drifting.
Reader, by way of moon, chance,
sun, circumstance, this is me
in your hands, unfolding.
We are on our final sets of teeth.
When you lose yours, I will
chew for the both of us.
We will swallow.
We will swallow it all down,
and be beautiful.

.   .   .

The winner makes a bet
ending in zero, one.

I was eleven when

mother revealed her crush

on Alex Trebek. Jeopardy

instantaneously becomes me

and this desire

to be a host of answers

awaiting the correct question.

Every decision silly and essential

as ones about facial hair.

Do, do, do, do…do, do, do.

I don't. Can't.

I've wagered modestly.

His trademark being what grows

from the center of the senses,

revelation of lip

is a reinvention. Stay tuned.

Jesus, sans beard.

Let me be perfectly clear

about this: When is an accent

earned? He could be

from anywhere and nowhere

at once. I was eleven

on the back of the bus,
a bubble inside the bubble
of my gum. Flavor strong,
doesn't last long.
Heather Pare—plaid skirt,
orangest red hair—unwrapped
a Starburst with her tongue
and my life
changed forever again.

.   .   .

We erred in naming
our ambition. It blew up
in our face. Challenger's
measurements were so complex
they were, practically speaking,
immeasurable. We know now
the less than perfect

mating surfaces were sealed
with a faulty ring.
Let us remember what was
lost, that grandeur
has enormous costs.
Shuttling from here to there,
there to here, let us be aware
what is done is
done in the name of Discovery.
January, the start of a new year.
I come to you humble
as a pair of crocheted mittens.

   •   •   •

Sometimes I must also tame
the lioness. Not with whip but by being
attentive to her movement
and demanding certain things.

Granted, it is posturing.

Both the top hat and the tails.

Two elephants stand tall on two legs;

a seal balances a beach ball on its nose.

So much of it really is about balancing.

The smallest wrong gesture

and we are out a limb.

The big top possible because the poles

extend. Living and being aware of it

is something like being knife

thrower and lovely assistant.

We let go as the wheel spins

with us tied to it. The dead are gone,

and the show must go on. Karl Wallenda,

I thought you brilliant

most of the afternoon, but realize now

you've gotten it wrong.

The dead are not gone

yet the show will go on.

These are only hints and guesses,

hints followed by guesses, and the rest

is prayer, observance, discipline,

thought and action.
Eliot said that. We went
from one side of the tightrope to the other,
stepped onto the pedestal and off
intentionally. Down we went
into the net where we are raised by biblical
fishermen. There is sunlight
on the water and on our
thin bodies, glistening. In the village,
a man cleans jewelry. Indeterminate amount
of shades in the mood ring.
The questions often point toward their answers.
We have so many ideas
we have no idea. I say let's make a decision
and go with it. We put in an application
for the cleanest, brightest, most spacious
space we can afford.
We of the poor and lacking
credit, we of the child and dog.
If what we submitted is not accepted,
someone else will move.
At some point we knew it.

The game began to end.
Hopefully it won't
soon. We will roll again,
new information crammed into
some crevice of our complicated brains.
Beneath the vehicle is a trap door
the clowns go in and out of
with ease. Perhaps
our shoes are too big to fill,
but if the flower of her lapel
squirts water into my eye,
may you be amused as I bend
toward it each subsequent time.

•   •   •

The child gives me every color
Starburst but red. I cannot
blame her, having

erased *all* preceding

my best at the end of a letter

to a friend. The uniformed exotic

woman demonstrates how

we should put on

our own masks

before helping others with theirs.

Before: the reason for

this putting on of masks.

She gives me half the can.

I want the whole thing.

Not thirsty at the moment,

confident I will be. We will be

late arriving. I offer no explanation

except the one offered me:

there were delays elsewhere

that caused our delays. Grounded,

in traffic I want

to warn the first rubber-necker,

Don't look. It's horrific.

The trapped passengers

bleeding, trapped, passengers.

The spider webbed windshield

not in the least bit

symbolic. He looks anyway.

Nearly wrote accept, not except.

Two things I remember most

from Driver's Ed: the dark curls

of that fair skinned girl,

an accident is always

more than one person's fault.

• • •

The Santa Fe rail never reached

Santa Fe. It's okay,

train. Few of us live up to

our name. Somewhere someone

drowns on a swallow that,

at the base of the right cactus,

could have been the desert

wanderer's life-saving sip.

We are here though, friends insist.

I tired of being a hobo.

One can only be thrown

from so many moving trains

before he stops hopping, hoping

all together. Crazy motives.

I took a white picket

fallen from the fence

after father left. I was playing war.

Andrew up the street

hypothetically shot me.

He said, you are dead,

but I was not dead. I was

angry. In a last ditch

effort for it not to end

like this, I threw that missing boundary,

a native's inadequate spear.

The calibers men are capable of

holding triggers our honor and

despair. The rusty nail that catches

the finger, and mother's countenance

dangling there. Bless the children

and their directness. Pity

the parents and their navigation systems.

Let us mull over the mule,

that emblem of explanation,

mare and ass offspring. On winter,

on. I feel best when alone

shoveling the drive of our rented home.

The woman, the child, the dog

inside, warm. Let me be out here,

the extent of valor extending

as far as the ferocity of any impending

storm. My muscle is my memory,

as gone is ingrained in the go.

Bend, lift, throw, Evan. Bend, lift, throw.

•   •   •

Crazy Horse was Sitting Bull's

right hand man. You chose to go

it alone. Nonetheless, in the end,

on your own terms, to go.

How you rode

in this new America—

helmet, Vespa. Contrary

to your insistence on late youth's

persistence, cautiousness crept up

on bravado. A man's man marked

by an ability to get away

with a purple coat.

This was always

the worthwhile trouble—

defining *with* given the going.

One night our class met

it was raining. After the routine

of cigarette and small talk

by manicured burly magnified,

you recited Byron. I remember

not how you got there

but that you said,

I wish I had a son.

Teacher, I have reached my twenty-ninth year

and still fear anything resembling

early absence. I fear you thus:

another father who is not, was.

A roving we go no more

given our eyes lower

in efforts at understanding.

Should it be held against you

that you pursued reactions from the beautiful

women in the room? You relished

being crude. Then, at the edge of unbearable,

left it. A dog tamed by his age,

you glanced at me, smirked

at the puff in my chest.

Infrequently these days

I return to those tables set together,

you at the head.

It is as if my classmates' young legs,

your legs worn so

soon to go lame, the solid legs

beneath the hard surface

where lines of your wisdom

were scrawled, sprawled across

the spiral bound—

it is as if all those legs

were my own now.

The wobble and the confidence

it will not collapse.

Your transparent desire to be accepted

as Alpha meows into present affection.

We did not know you,

but the you we knew, we loved.

Soon after hearing

the news of your death,

standing, heads bent, retriever

eyes growing calmly wild,

we made a pact:

If ever one of us feels

the way you must have felt,

we will let the others know.

Liam, Prodigal, Executive Director

relentlessly conscious

of position and power,

the catch with even the strongest will

is that what we call ourselves

holds weight only if embraced

by those that follow.

•   •   •

I find the toucan encouraging.

Black body, colorful beak.

Most of the time though,

I am Mike Collins.

While Buzz and Neil made their way

to certain impressions, he was the guy

circling the moon at a distance.

Weightless aside from the wanting

to touch down. Christin, can we?

To say my name

and everything that means was here.

Markings on a stall wall. Truth is,

I just want to put my flag

in something. We came all this way

but what will we have

to show for it? The bird

said follow your nose.

The dog keeps sniffing around.

What if he meant *knows*?

I want us in an airy lockstep

but can't get a foothold

on the simple pleasure of birdsong.

I head to the field

guide in search of an image and name

for the source of any sound.

I'm up the whole night

watching infomercials.

The swimming pool you swim in

without going anywhere does not appeal to me.

I'm considering how much I need

a knife that can cut through change

given we're typically broke

but have been making

an effort to maintain a basket full of fruit.

It has gotten to the point now

in the wee hours

when she and I are in separate rooms

the dog doesn't know what to do.

.   .   .

Aside from the dividers

in place to keep apart

the parts we will become,

we began empty. Aside from

the color we chose

or were designated, we began

empty. Aside from the inherent

shape and the shapes within

that shape, we began empty.
There is always room for more.
My sister, Maura, was given
More as a nickname. Moore:
Why should honour outlive honesty?
I speak on behalf
of the mothballs
buried in mother's mother's chest.
As a toddler, Christin's brother
could not pronounce her name, so
he called her Kinkin, which was
shortened to Kin.
She does not speak to her family.
She does not feel well today.
I touch a cool, damp cloth
to her forehead.
I say, here you are, Kin,
turning her discomfort
into my own happiness
into my own discomfort
with the pleasure
we take in taking care.

• • •

Today the world is surprised
a killer whale killed its trainer.
He turned over and over for her
for years before turning on her.
What should we make of it? Many of us
won't get in the tank but hope the splash
reaches our row. I think
Sea World is one of those places
you should dream of but never go.
The buildup and the letdown.
Polaris, a constant star, was
the standard for second magnitude
brightness until astronomers discovered
its brightness varies over time.
Today's building is tomorrow's ruin.
Fear. Fear not.
From ruin arises more possibility.
What makes the crane remarkable

is its capacity to rise and plunge.
I read there is a magnetic pull
keeping everything separate.
So, for example, when you
sit in a chair you are actually hovering.
It looks like we are touching,
but we are not touching.

•   •   •

Honorable, or moron spectacle?
Sticking it out or flat out stuck?
Craig MacTavish was the last
NHL player to play without helmet.
Motorcycle on a road of minivans.
We're the ones who will hit him
then know the hearse hurt. I'm pissed,
which is easier to say than scared
I'm not more like him. She wants

to walk out on the ice. I say
hell no; she and the dog go.
As a boy, chose the lowest limb
of the climbing tree
but sat so often, so steady,
I wore it thin. Jennifer says there's more
than one, more than two
ways to live. Reckless or wreck less—
father, mother—I try my best to remember
and reconcile. Spectacles
are seeing improvers, assuming
one perception's truer than another.
I am reading an origami instruction book
backwards. I am unfolding
every angle, decreasing to widen
into one fell swoop of song—every inch
of ebbing, enormity of calm.
Let swan be sand and sky, pond.

•   •   •

Yeats had it right:

cloak, boat, shoes—all

sorrow. Draped, decked, laced

in song. Brother's friend

built an instrument so big

its notes could only be

felt. Manually powered

fastener-driving impact device.

This is what the Department of Defense calls

a hammer. Applied, we're supporting

a structure: from would to beam.

Split, nailed, splintered. We are splintered.

The smallest things get under our skin.

I remember as a boy

crying about one

so much mother handed me

the sewing needle—*Dig it out.*

This is what the base coach says

to the runner who will not be safe.

Christin and I arrive home

within minutes of each other but not

at exactly the same time.

Similar, separate unlocking, locking.

Each of us went to the store.

She unpacks the fruits I'd forgotten.

I, the grains she overlooked.

We both anticipated future spilling.

Resplendent the abode

of my Brawny and her Bounty.

The desire to go

from one who rents to one who owns

rises like water in the shared shower

we rarely share since the one the other made

plans to see became that somebody always there.

Ask me—the cause is fallen

strands of her before

all around me hair. We are clumped

together now, ugly or not.

I am unsure

which is the worst form of narcissism:

singing oneself or thinking we

know the lyrics to anything else.

The leaves are grateful

to the rake. The log

cabin, the lake.

Some use rope to climb,

others to tie things down.

The hood of my Legacy

flew up out of nowhere.

I was in the middle of nowhere.

The windshield smashed. I thought not

of mother or Christin, but peered

calmly through a crack,

pulled myself to the closest shoulder.

Alive and overdramatic,

I tell her I can't stand

those Tarzan-esque tops

some ladies wear.

It feels so imbalanced.

Me Tarzan, you Jane.

Me pedestrian, you tank.

The shocks were next to go.

Every pothole became a crater.

Then, love—oh dearest, dearest

love—when you, the child, and I

were working in the yard,

I felt so full of the fall

I swore not all the dead

in the world could diminish

our aliveness. The three of us

there, clearing what was

for what will become.

The dog scratching at the window.

Your feeling bad for him.

The child's feeling bad for him.

Our allowing him

one final romp in the piles

before we lined tall paper bags

along the curbside

and a wind

had them lean

on each other.

.   .   .

In basketball, the hesitation,

also known as the stutter step,

is one of the simplest

yet most effective moves

a player can make.

It is about illusion, elusion, and pace.

The idea is to get the person

staying with you

thinking they are right with you.

You act like you are going

but you are not going.

Just like that, you're gone.

When surfaced, the actual

size of a two-by-four is one

and a half by three and a half inches.

I've never felt comfortable rounding

numbers. My graph paper

would have so many lines

the whole thing would be blue.

We are back where we started.

The actual resurfaces

among new inaccuracies.

Part of me wants to stay

for the final minutes

regardless of the discrepancy.

We paid to be here.

If we leave now,

and they come back, we will miss

one of the greatest triumphs

in the history of the game.

When you block someone out

you do not allow them

to gain the inside position.

The parquet in the original Garden

was famously uneven.

Pieces of the old surface

are interspersed in the new.

When this game is over

they will pick up the floor

and lay down ice in its place.

.   .   .

Leaving, she leaves construction
paper on the windowsill.
It takes days and inattention
to realize the colors fade.
In contrast, the sun makes me
absurdly vibrant. Whenever
anyone touches me,
it hurts. Friend, we try to take
solace in the solstice, in defining
moments that dictate
duration, yet her breasts are still filling
with milk, Mei Yao Ch'en says
of the mother whose newborn
has died. Natives named the canyon
House of Stone and Light.
Passage to a Venice prison
was known as the Bridge of Sighs.
Authentic places turn to tourist destinations.

I feel like an asshole

when I say anything.

An American with no claim

to the land he was born in

speaking Spanish imitating an Italian

accent. Visiting the Vatican, I wanted

to declare myself

an independent nation.

Then I thought of her,

I thought of you, dear reader.

I thought of history

and the other categories that merge

upon our embarkation. The wheel

of successes and failures

where worth requires

pronouncement, witness.

God bless America!

There is an abundance

of pie pieces. There are wedges

cut to fit perfectly

between floors and doors.

·   ·   ·

And the quiet of love
in her feet—Yeats again.
The dog bows beneath her
hand so she has no choice
but to touch him.
By ten, Ivan was already
chucking puppies off the wall.
But when did he become
Terrible? Evan the Intelligible
I'd like to be called.
More so, I'd like to be felt.
So itself I'd love
to tell: There will be recourse
when you allow actions
independence. Allow actions
independence. The dog keeps
looking out the window
and crying. What city please?

Grandmother was an operator

but that job's nearly

obsolete. Neighbors

on all sides, sometimes

I think we've become

too close to get any closer.

Drop the puppy, Ivan.

It comes down to understanding:

the course of history recoursing.

If the girl wants

to be forgotten, forget

the girl. Walk yourself

weary, Evan. Return to a master

at whose feet you can curl.

·   ·   ·

I know joy the way the grounded

do watching loved ones climb limbs:

proud, privy to catastrophe.

I thought steadfast and stable

the oath of the oak's trunk

before happening with tired feet

upon the facility of stump.

There are many uses for hair elastics.

My favorite is their acting as enablers

of viewing a particular woman

dipping her head and raising her hands

in sunlight. We are aware

of the particles that make up dust dancing

magically, momentarily

between layers. It is not that

my heart lacks the anchor's heft,

but more, how a body of water

cinches the sunken object.

There is a swimming pool

inside the concrete building.

We take steel wool to the sink.

The child thinks rust a losing.

I tell her in softer terms,

it is an adding on

of the unwanted.

She asks why

should she make the bed

if it'll get messed up again.

The man pulled over

for driving in the carpool lane

with a blowup doll in the front seat

spoke not of loneliness,

but of a need to be somewhere.

Only five months

now before I will owe

brother that hundred dollars.

You can't teach height, he told me

repeatedly. I stretched myself in doorframes,

made marks on their interiors.

Brother, thank you for this comfort I take in

measuring myself against anything.

Whitman and Dickinson,

dust and rust, can't and won't, must.

Our neighbors placed one spotlight on a tree,

another on the flag of our country.

Anything at half mast spangles

with quiet remembrance, sad. Mass,
dad. How childish! How unacceptably
self-conscious! I have traveled
to distant lands. There is only
one way to reach any state
beyond that which we are born into:
realizing self, give it to someone else.
Child, little sparrow in the highest tree,
here is my great joy and sorrow.
Forgive the world and me.

.   .   .

The avocado ripens in the dark
the paper provides. I had forgotten
how quickly. The opportunity
it had to be most delicious
is lost. From gleaming to spotty.
So much comes down

to timing. The fastest man

on the planet's slow goodbye.

Today his name is Usain—pronounced

You sane—Bolt.

I don't know what to believe

is real anymore. The day will come.

His record will be broken

in record time. The toddler drops the doll,

stretches an adamant arm:

Come back, come back.

The fingers opening and closing

with inexperience. The mother trusts

no doll can return itself.

She picks it up.

The eyes blink. No one is astonished.

Headphones get more and more

discrete, but those I know

with an ear for music insist on

the gray and gaudy.

Some qualities cannot be compromised.

The wingéd masses must be

guided to the gates.

Neither taking off nor landing,

but taxiing causes the most

tire wear. Motion made the doll

lifelike. The boy throws her to the ground

this time, laughing. It would be sinister

if he knew all the implications.

Unknowingly wise treating the empty

handed and handed back

as a game. If no one reads

my poems, I will bury them

in the grave of my love,

ala Dante Gabrielle Rossetti.

The editor says it was exaggerated

remorse and sentimental self-

sacrifice. I try to avoid

the category of history

all together. So many questions

I can't answer. Sometimes

the roll of the die,

the places I have already been

leave me no choice but to go

to that yellow space

where the blondest lady

in the bluest bikini

walked along Narragansett

pier. Father told us

of the other woman

then and there. She was not her

but always will be. I never noticed

the face. The shape though,

that shape. My favorite instrument became

the triangle. I stood at

attention, reluctant to chime in.

My favorite triangle became the isosceles,

and the world thought it strange

that I should prefer one triangle to another.

World, this is the way the world works. I turn

my rejection slips into snowflakes.

I take off my sweater

in the sunlight. It's not summer yet

says the stranger with the gaps

in his teeth. No kidding.

Christin may or may not want me.

I am making plans anyway.

I will name my first born Samaritan
and hope he turns out good.

ACKNOWLEDGEMENTS

Grateful acknowledgement is given to the editors of
the following journals where selections from this
poem first appeared, sometimes in slightly different
forms.

Arch Literary Journal: "All I had to do was keep
turning"; "A telephone pole covered"

H_NGM_N: "Edwin Budding invented the
lawnmower."; "Needles pushed into a pillow";
"Posing a higher risk"; "Galileo measured moon
mountains"; "We begin by claiming a color."

Michigan Quarterly Review: "They were perfectly fine"
(as "A Framed Absence")

Thank you to the following friends and poets, all of
whom helped make this book possible: Jackie Clark,
Jennifer H. Fortin, P.J. Gallo, Christie Ann Reynolds,
Hilary Russell, Barry Sternlieb, Paige Taggart, Jason
Ueda. Special thanks to Yotam Hadass for believing in
this poem when no one else seemed to, and for
making suggestions that improved it. Thanks to Nate
Pritts, Scott O'Connor, and the H_NGM_N editorial
board. Thank you to Jennifer Michael Hecht and
Matthew Zapruder. Love and love and thanks and
thanks to my family, especially my mother, Christin,
and Chase.

Evan Glasson was born in Providence, RI and lives in Arlington, MA. His poems have appeared in *Barrow Street*, *Hanging Loose*, *Michigan Quarterly Review*, and *Poetry East*, among others. He holds an MFA from the New School, where he was a Riggio Writing and Democracy Initiative Teaching Fellow. He has worked at the National Book Foundation, and as a high school and college English teacher. In 2008, he received a Travel to the Collections Award from the Smithsonian Institution's Lemelson Center for the Study of Invention and Innovation. He co-edits the poetry journal, *LEVELER*.

14342794R00058

Made in the USA
Charleston, SC
06 September 2012